beginning to see

a collection of epigrams
about the problem
of living

and the freedom
to be gained
through meditation

by sujata

pen-art by julio lynch

Apple Pie Books
san francisco

Library of Congress Cataloging
    In publication Data
Sujata, 1948
    Beginning to See
    1. Psychology 2. Epigrams, English.
    I. Title.
    BQ5612.S9 1981 294.3'443   81-4681
    ISBN   0-913300-06-3

printed in the united states
of america

beginning to see

this book is dedicated to

the 9 to 5ers.
and everybody else

much suffering
comes into the
life of one who
tries to be any-
where but
  here
in the present
moment

are you
content
with where you
are right now?

because "right nows" are all you have

there is nothing
in this life that we can
have for very long

things and people
come ...
                 then leave us ...

and we are left
sad and aching
because of
our
attachment

because we are only
accepting of pleasure
in our lives

an immense
amount of fear
is created as
we spend our
lives dodging
pain

an immense amount
of fear is created
as we spend our lives
dodging pain

an immense amount
of fear is created
as we spend our
lives dodging pain

the world continually
demands that we
direct our
attention
outside
ourselves

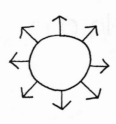

meditation teaches
us to revolt

and turn that
awareness toward
our neglected
dimly-lit
insides ...

Painful feelings*
in the mind indicate
wrong attitudes
about life

a meditation
retreat can show
us what we're
doing wrong

*jealousy, envy, hatred, loneliness, frustration, depression

we live our
lives fearfully

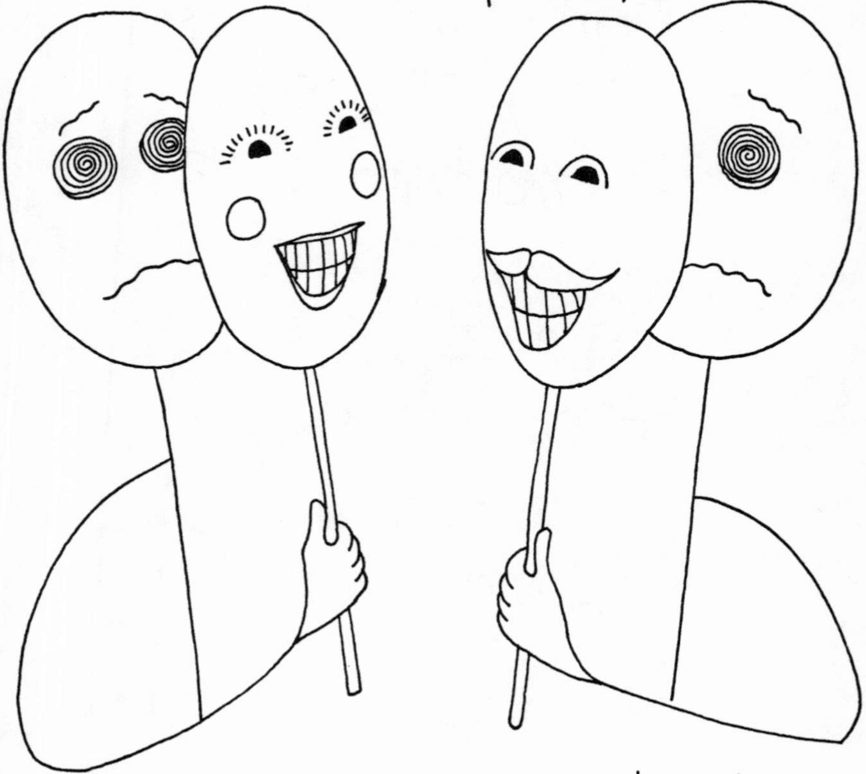

to such an extent
that we live
dishonestly

there is dishonesty

in any mind

which demands

that reality

occur in a

specific way

we progress in this
life according to our
honest wisdom.

honest wisdom is
realizing what you feel,
knowing what you think,
and opening
your attention
   to everything
      which comes
         before you.

We should take
time each day to
understand
ourselves
        to watch exactly
    what we experience
    in walking and sitting
        meditation.

every day you are
responsible
for how you feel

no one can make you
unhappy
or nervous

choices in a
meditator's life are
very simple:

he does those
things which contribute
to his awareness

he refrains from
things which do not

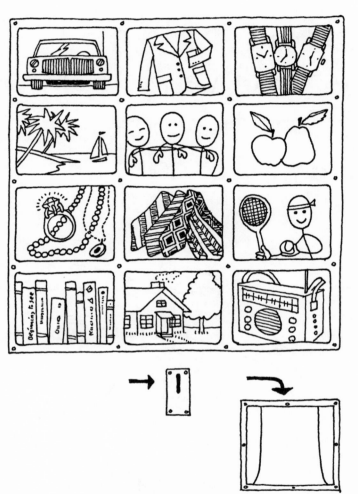

the first step in
spiritual growth is to
do what we love to do
and to become
aware of doing it

in what direction
are you taking yourself?
(is it worth your effort?
is it exactly where
you want
to go?)

Coolsville
Worryhollow
Fun City
Worktown
Twinkyland
Restrooms

insight meditation
systematically trains us
to be aware of every-
thing "we're up to"

the mind is only a
sophisticated
mirror

it is what it sees
it is what it sees

be careful what
you show it because
you can be

anything
anything
anything
anything

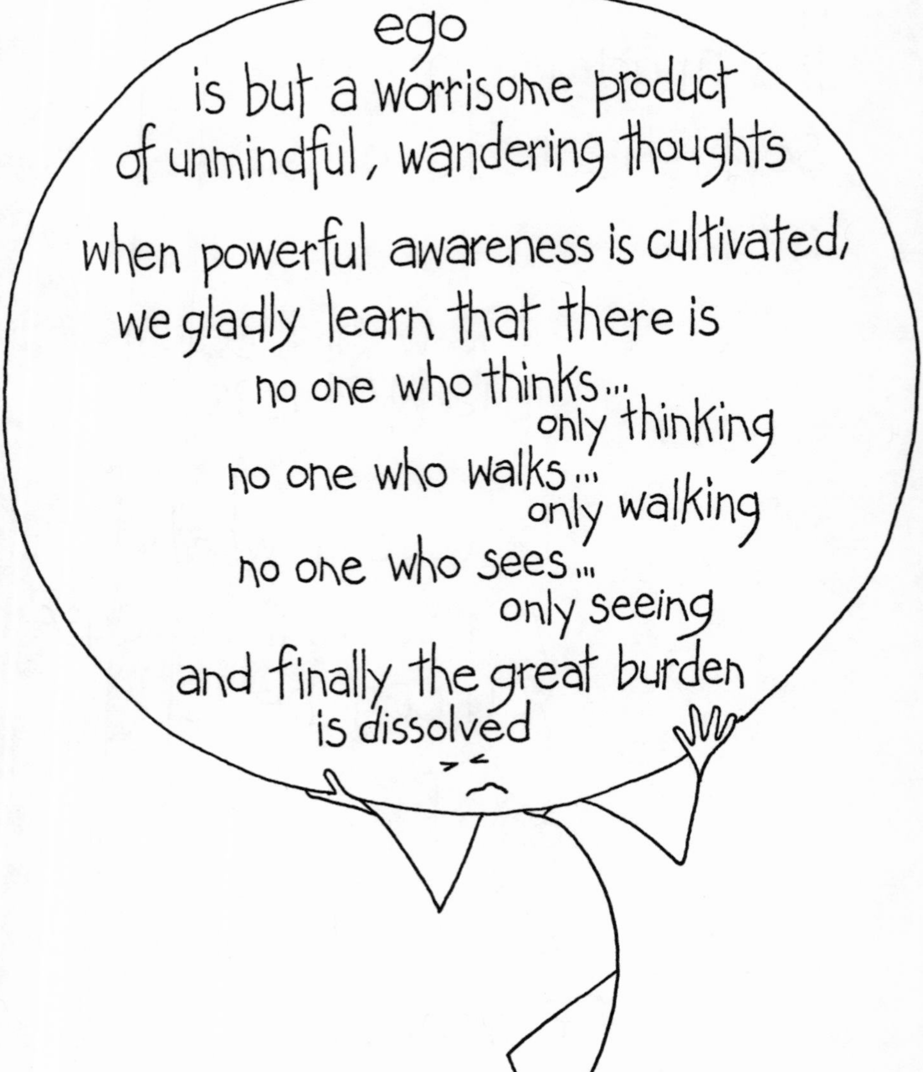

ego
is but a worrisome product
of unmindful, wandering thoughts
when powerful awareness is cultivated,
we gladly learn that there is
no one who thinks...
only thinking
no one who walks...
only walking
no one who sees...
only seeing
and finally the great burden
is dissolved

detached
does not mean
dead

rather, it is made of

Lovingkindness

Compassion

Sympathetic joy

and

equanimity

one of the
highest blessings is
a friend with whom
we can respond
openly and freely

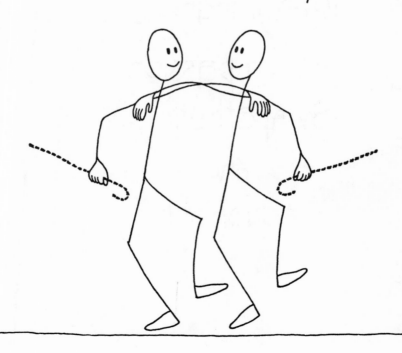

it is hard
to be constantly
loving

but it is
harder
to be
unloving

this living is
so hard
how can we
be anything
but loving?

    besides teaching insight meditation the buddha also taught a meditation to develop loving kindness for all creatures — he instructed that we sit in a quiet place and reflect first on the dangers of hatred, anger and resentment, and the benefits of loving kindness — these reflections remind us of the importance of maintaining a loving attitude in all circumstances and give us energy for the meditation.

    because only when there is love for one-self can there be love for others, we first practice lovingkindness towards ourselves by thinking of our own good qualities and kind actions — warmth for ourselves grows as we repeat over and over the loving thought: 'may I be free from my troubles (anger, fear, tension, anxiety, hatred, etc.) may I live happily.'

    when we first begin the practice of loving-kindness, we may be surprised to find that we have difficulty in reflecting on our good qualities — we may feel shy or guilty in thinking of ourselves in such a positive way, or there may be self-hatred conditioned in our minds by years of comparing ourselves with others or with some ideal to which we might cling.

    when we begin practice, it may be helpful to start each period of practice by writing down a few reflections to help us focus our attention.

    for example, one day our reflections might be:

dangers of hatred and resentment

1- makes me fearful
2- creates restlessness and agitation
3- makes me feel miserable
4- makes me critical and hard on myself

advantages of lovingkindness

1- makes my mind clear
2- frees my body of tension
3- makes me feel good about myself
4- makes it easier to be with others

my own good qualities

1- I try to be patient
2- I am willing to change and grow
3- I want to be more loving
4- I have pretty toes

spend some time each day writing and reflecting in this way - then spend the last ten minutes of the meditation time specifically cultivating that warm and open space which thoughts of lovingkindness produce, by gently and silently repeating your own wish for yourself : 'may I be loving' or 'may I be free from restlessness' or 'may I be free from anxiety,' in whatever way feels appropriate for you.

if we work ardently at this meditation we will begin to see a healthy change happening within ourselves.

in time, when loving thoughts flow freely for ourselves, the lovingkindness may be extended to all beings everywhere without distinction —

may all beings be happy.

anger is most
dangerous

it destroys you,
the person next
to you,
and the place where
you live

when aversion arises in
our minds,
we must either mindfully
drop it
or start communicating

hatred
is a crime
  in any of its forms--
    resentment, aversion,
  jealousy, anger, harshness,
      disgust--

    if we watch carefully
  what it does to our
  feelings and what we do
  to other peoples feelings
 when motivated by it, we
  have no choice but to
    give it up

we are very empty inside
just watch us work to fill
up the vacant hours

time on our
hands is very
dangerous

we might stop long
enough to notice that
we are very unhappy
people
          going nowhere
          special .....

the buddha did not
come in the 6th
century b.c.

to reassure us
that
the world was
moving in the
right
direction

Once a King who was march-
ing to war came near the place
where an enlightened teacher was
living. the King was in a great
hurry but he wanted to learn
something from the saint. respectfully the King approached, paid
homage, and asked the holy one:

"will you tell me the buddha's
teachings, for I have little time and
may even be killed this very day"

the sage looked upon the
man in the royal cloak and answer-
ed with but one word:

"awareness"

meditation is
for those who are
born without having
it all together

mindfully attending to the sensation
of the breath -
a tranquility and insight exersise -

is politically, economically
and spiritually
the practice
of
peacefulness

meditation is not straining
or striving

it is a relaxation

the back should be straight
not tense

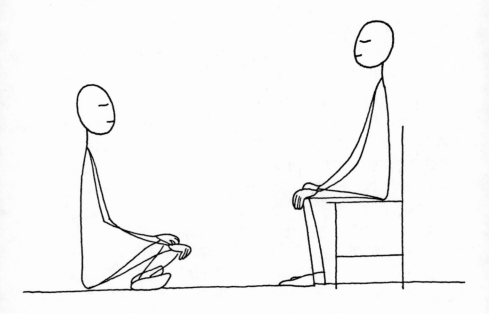

an insight
meditation exercise

for the development of clear, mindful awareness, the buddha taught us to observe closely the movements of the body and the mind. a good way to develop your attentiveness, concentration and insight is to watch carefully the rising and falling of the abdomen. in this meditation exercise we begin by observing these obvious bodily movements. when these become clear we will also be able to be aware of the more subtle movements of the mind.

go to a quiet place and sit in a comfortable position with eyes closed and back straight but not rigid. the movement of the abdomen is always present: place your attention on its natural in and out movement, making a mental note of each part of the process as it is occurring. it is not necessary to verbally repeat the words, "rising" and "falling", or even to think of "rising" and "falling" in the form of words. instead, only be aware of the actual process of rising and falling. as you become more and more alert and can follow the movements more carefully, you will become aware that the breathing is sometimes shallow, sometimes deep, sometimes rapid, sometimes slow and calm. these variations should be noted, however there should be no effort to control or to interfere with the breathing in any way. just choicelessly watch the movements as they appear when you are breathing normally.

while you are watching the rise and fall of the abdomen, the mind may, by itself, go towards other objects, such as thoughts, feelings, bodily sensations. these new objects should be noted as soon as they arise. if a thought comes to your mind, be aware of "thinking". if a sound comes to your attention, make a mental note of "hearing". after each such note, firmly and calmly return your attention to the primary objects of meditation, the movements of the abdomen.

as you develop more concentration on the primary objects, you will quickly notice any other object as it arises. however, until the mind is alert enough to notice these objects as soon as they arise, it will tend to wander unmindfully after these thoughts, feelings and emotions. sometime later, the meditator becomes aware that he has been day dreaming. as soon as one is aware that his attention has drifted away from the present moment, he should patiently note that his mind has been "wandering" and that he is now "remembering to be mindful". then one should lovingly return the attention to watching the rising and falling.

mindfulness can also be practiced during walking meditation, with the lifting, placing and putting of the foot as the primary objects of awareness. with head upright, keeping your eyes on the ground about six feet ahead, walk at a moderately slow pace, with steps small enough so that, without losing your balance, you can place one foot firmly on the ground before moving the next foot. remember to note each part of the movement as it occurs. it is a good idea to spend equal amounts of time in walking and in sitting meditation --- for example, thirty minutes of walking, then thirty of sitting, later, one hour of walking, then one hour of sitting.

during all movements and activities of the day --- eating, washing, moving from place to place, job to job --- one should be aware of the movements of the body necessary for each activity, or of any thought, feeling or physical sensation which arises predominately.

one who persists in noting all objects as they come to his attention will develop increasingly clear awareness. noting should be done neither too fast nor too slowly. It should be immediate, firm and clear, but not harsh. one is not to be lazy and sit day dreaming, but rather to develop an awareness of the objects which is accepting and alert. at a certain point when the mindfulness is well developed, awareness will be automatic, and there will be less and less need for making mental notes. however, whenever attention weakens, one should return to making clear notes.

it would be convenient if one could simply "decide" to be aware. however, we are conditioned not to be aware. our minds

are trained to be complicated, and so it is necessary to re-train ourselves in order to be simply
aware. the most skillful way for a beginning
meditator to develop mindful awareness is to
place himself under the guidance of a qualified
meditation teacher for a period of intense
practice. during a meditation retreat one leaves
behind for a time the rush and trouble of his
daily life, and in an atmosphere of quiet mindfulness and lovingkindness, devotes his energy
entirely to the development of awareness. the
minimum length of time usually needed for
beginning westerners is one month. after
completing such a period of intensive meditation, one is better able to continue the development and practice of mindfulness in daily life.

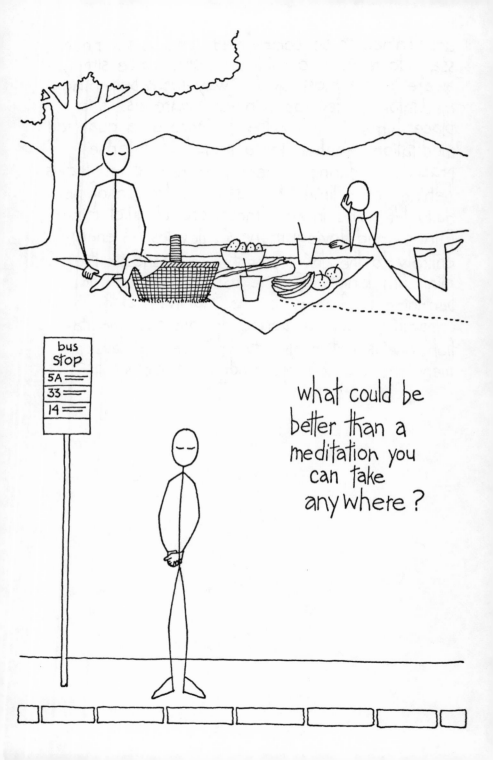

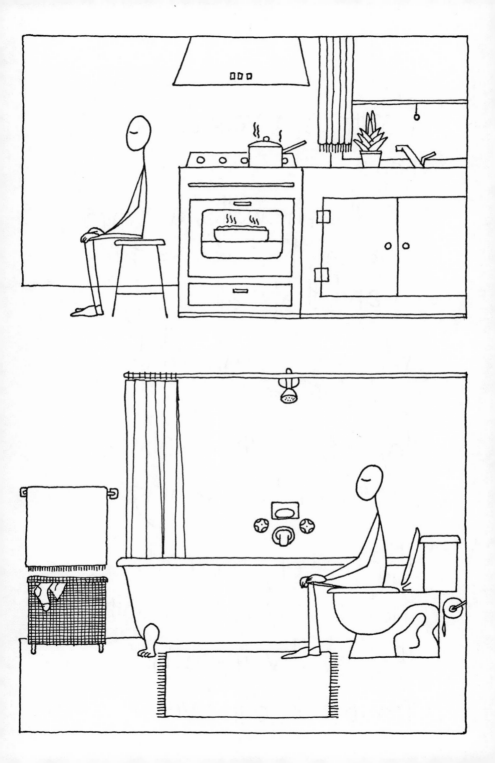

a saint is a very simple
man:
    when he walks, he walks
    when he talks, he talks
    and thats all
he doesn't think while
    listening,
day dream while walking
    see while touching

that is very hard
that is why he is a saint
that is why there is
trouble in our lives

tension
is the first noble truth:

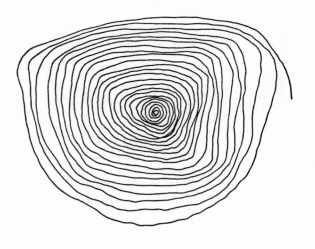

life is suffering

the price of
wisdom
is pain:

but it is this wisdom
that cuts off
the suffering

finally, there is
no choice but
to bleed freely

Your pain can be
the breaking
of the shell
which
encloses
your
under-
standing

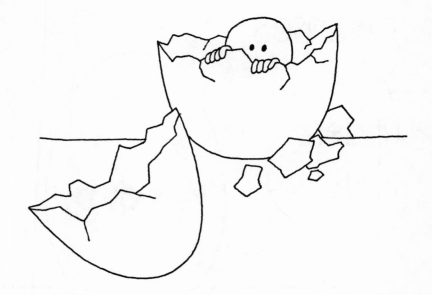

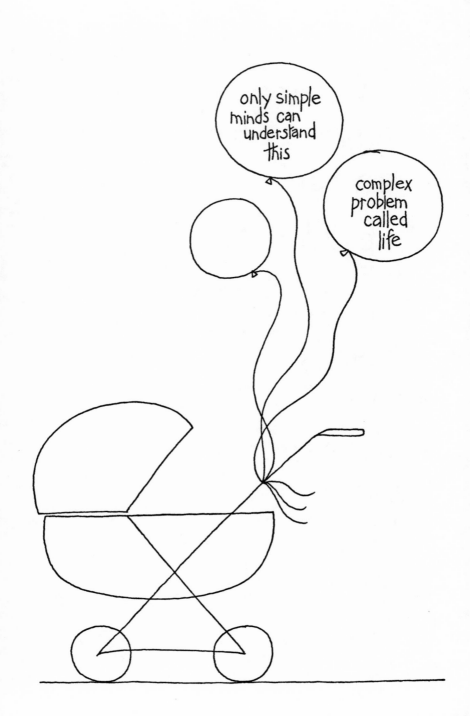

if we accept everything
in life as our
teacher

we will soon
be free

from the
pain of
unnecessary resistance
and
unnecessary desire

we run here and there
all our lives
trying to be successful,
    correct and right

when the
    goal
    of life
    is
learning

meditation does not necessarily make us feel good but it does awaken us to the many things we do feel

a meditation retreat
brings great relief because
for a time we don't have
to take our mind and its'
problems seriously,

we don't have to act
upon its thousand wander-
ing thougts,

we just note them
mindfully and they pass
away . . . .

the untrained
mind is so
vulnerable to
   circumstances

something good
happens and it
is happy...

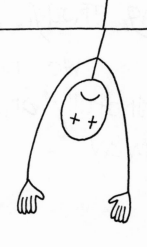

something bad
happens and it
is in pain...

one who has sufficiently
suffered the attachments
and aversions of his mind's
uncontrolled wanderings
quickly becomes

watchful ⟨◦ ◦⟩ of

any direction ⟨◦ ◦⟩

in which ⟨◦ ◦⟩

⟨◦ ◦⟩ the mind

⟨◦ ◦⟩ moves

Your mind has
a mind of its
own

(where
do
You
 fit in ?)

thoughts are not
necessarily connected
with reality

   that is why the
buddha taught us
to be aware
of them
before we are
influenced
by them

what happens between
the time we awake
and the time we
go to bed

is out
of our control

bittersweet goes the life of him —
that clouded and distracted
stranger to reality
without awareness, he
stumbles and falls
he hurts himself to death

the mind is the
only means we have
of getting out of
this mess

careful
with it

immorality
selfishness,
anger and
chemicals
dull this single key

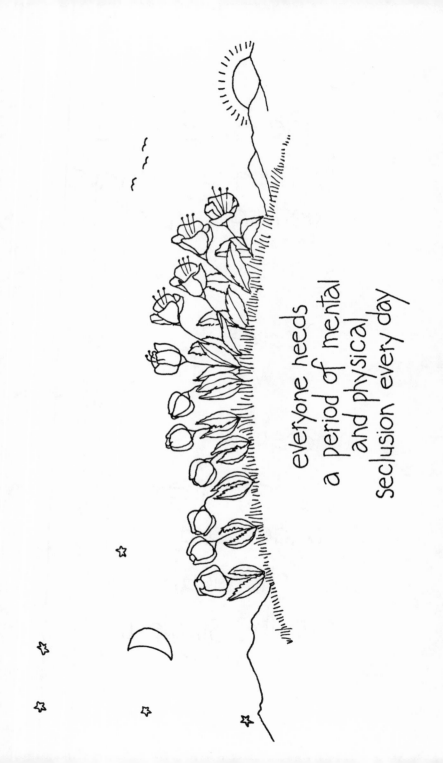

everyone needs
a period of mental
and physical
seclusion every day

meditating is
the kindest
thing we can
do for
ourselves

our mind is a
garden
by selecting
what it thinks
upon,

we can grow
either
thorny weeds
or beautiful
tender flowers

(but even a
little weed
can learn
to grow
flowers)

reaching
enlightenment
is just a matter
of continuous
practice . . . . ✳

you can

do

it

our characters are
developed by persistent practice

if we practice love
we become more loving

if we practice patience
we become more patient

if we practice generosity
we become more generous

communication loving kindness
insight into reality

form an interdependent
triangle :

neglect one and we
diminish the other two
practice one and all
are increased

basically
life is unsatisfactory
because:

1. it is not perfect
2. we only get two weeks of vacation
   each year
3. our joys are impermanent
4. no one gets out alive
5. our bodies have to be washed over
   and over again
6. the freeway is crowded
7. we must be taught by pain as well
   as by pleasure
8. our name sounds dumb
9. we must argue that life is not
   unsatisfactory
10. most of our happiness depends
    on mere thoughts of the past
    and the future

mindfulness is
the cure for the
disease of
suffering

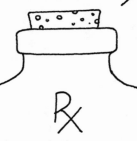

Rx

mindfulness

keep within
reach of everyone

take delight in mindfulness,
control your mind,
pull yourself
out of the mire of passions

as would an elephant
sunk in mud
come out of it

nothing is gained without effort
to train your mind, you have to work
every minute, every day, every year

from one life to another

be kind and merciful
let no one ever come to you
without going away
better and happier

mercy is the highest
attitude

one day a mother lost her only child. she went to
the buddha in search of a remedy for her dead
son, carrying the corpse. the buddha agreed to
help her if she could bring to him a bag of
white mustard seeds. however, she had to obtain
these mustard seeds from a house where no
member had ever died.
the distraught mother went from one house to

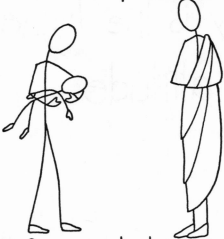

another asking if anyone had ever died in the
house. the answer was always positive... here the
grandfather died 3 years ago, - there the mother
died by giving birth to her last child, etc...
in every house she was told: "the living are few,
but the dead are many".

after a while she understood the nature of life.
she returned to the buddha without the
mustard seeds . the buddha comforted her
explaining that death is common to all living
beings.
she understood that the life of human beings
flickers like the light of the lamp and she
finally stopped weeping and accepted the
death of her only son.

to tomb to tomb to tomb to tomb to womb to tomb to tomb to womb to tomb to womb to tomb to tomb to womb to tomb to womb to tomb to womb to tomb to tomb to womb to tomb to womb to tomb to tomb to womb to tomb to tomb to womb to tomb to womb to tomb to tomb to womb to tomb to womb to tomb to womb to tomb to womb to tomb to tomb to womb to tomb to womb to tomb to womb to tomb to womb to tomb to womb to tomb to tomb to womb to tomb to womb to tomb to womb to tomb to womb to tomb

enlightment is an
alternative
to life, after life, after
life, after life, after
life, after life, after
life, after life, after life,
after life, after life, after life, after life, after life, after life, after life, after life, after life, after life, after life, after life

During the time of the buddha, there was a young monk called nanda who did not understand the necessity for mindfulness. one day, nanda began to cherish the idea of giving his best robe to the enlightened teacher sangara.
nanda was most infatuated with the idea, thinking that it would be an act of great merit to show such generosity towards a spiritually developed being.

he thought to himself, "by this noble deed, surely I will soon attain enlightment". because he was not yet well trained to mindfully watch the nature of his thoughts, nanda did not recognize the selfish desire and attachment which made his intentions impure.

the next day, the young monk waited until sangara left the monastery. in his absence, nanda swept his room, brought water for drinking and washing, prepared a seat for him of cushions and flowers, and laid out the gift of the robe. then nanda sat down and waited. when he saw sangara returning, he quickly went out the road, greeted him respectfully, and brought him to his quarters. seeing the room, the teacher was pleased with the young monks energy and kindness. nanda invited him to be seated on the prepared seat, gave him water to drink, bathed his feet. then nanda took a palm leaf and began to fan the holy one. he began the presentation of the gift, saying that he wanted with all his heart to give this, his best robe, to sangara.

the teacher detected that the young monk had not been mindful of his desires and had allowed

if living were an easy
thing to do
there would be no need
for mental training

but because life often

becomes very,
very hard

we often have
to meditate
very, very
hard

himself to become attached to the idea of giving this gift . seeing this as an opportunity to teach nanda the danger of unmindfulness, the holy one replied that he already had a complete set of robes and as he had no need for the gift, instructed nanda to give the robe to some needy monk. at this nanda repeated his request several times, only to have the teacher thank him for offering the gift, but instruct him to give it elsewhere .

this polite refusal hurt nanda's feelings and resentment arose in his mind . in this clouded state of mind, he stood fanning the teacher. rather than practicing mindfulness by dismissing his resentment and attending to the fanning, nanda permitted his mind to dwell on the incident . as his mind wandered concerning the declined gift, his resentment grew, and he thought,

"if sangara is not willing to recieve my gift, why should I remain a monk ? I will become a householder once more". then his thoughts began to wander restlessly, taking his attention farther and farther from the present moment in which he stood fanning the teacher.

"suppose I become a householder once more", he thought, "how shall I earn a living ? I will sell this robe and buy myself a she-goat. as the she-goat brings forth young, I will sell them and in this way make a profit. when I have accumulated a profit, I will take a wife, and my wife will bear me a son. I will put my son in a little cart, and taking my son and wife along with me, I will make the journey back here to pay respects to the elder sangara. as we travel, I will say to my wife, "wife, bring my son, for I wish to carry him. she will reply," why should you carry the boy? you push the cart". saying this, she will take the boy in her arms, thinking to carry him herself; but lacking the necessary strength, she will let him fall in the road and he will land in the path of the wheels and the cart will run over him. then I will say to her, "wife, you have ruined me". so saying I will bring down my stick upon her head".

so pondered nanda as he stood fanning the elder. consumed by his reflections, he swung his palm-leaf fan and brought it down on the head of the elder. sangara considered within himself "why has nanda struck me on the head?" immediately becoming aware of every thought which had passed through the mind of his attendant, he said to him, "nanda, you did not succeed in hitting the woman, but what has an old teacher done to deserve a beating? the young monk thought to himself, "I am in disgrace! the elder knows the foolish thoughts which have passed through my mind."

the teacher told nanda that if he sought forgiveness he should come and sit before him. trembling, nanda sat down, his eyes cast upon the floor he had so proudly swept a short time before.

sangara spoke quietly and patiently, "nanda,

do you see that you have made no effort to mindfully watch your thoughts, and do you see how needlessly you have suffered because of your mind's unwatched wanderings.

"your gift was not freely given because you demanded that it be recieved in a specific way. when your demands were unfulfilled you suffered resentment. the resentment was allowed to grow unwatched until it had made you completely unmindful. as you stood fanning me, you negligently became absorbed in wandering thoughts which had nothing to do with the present moment.

"do you see now the danger of unmindful thinking? do you see that if the mind is not carefully watched, one will become painfully absorbed in unwholesome states of mind? one unwholesome mental state weakens the mind so that it becomes susceptible to another and another. in this way, your mind, weakend by selfish desires, became caught in attachment, which led to disappointment, resentment, delusion and now regret.

"nanda, work gently and persistently to develop the mindfulness. as you have seen, one who does not live each moment in mindful awareness is bound for one painful experience after another. he who learns to watch the restless cravings and painful attachments of the mind will soon give up the suffering".

the innocent mind is willing to try anything... just because of its innocence

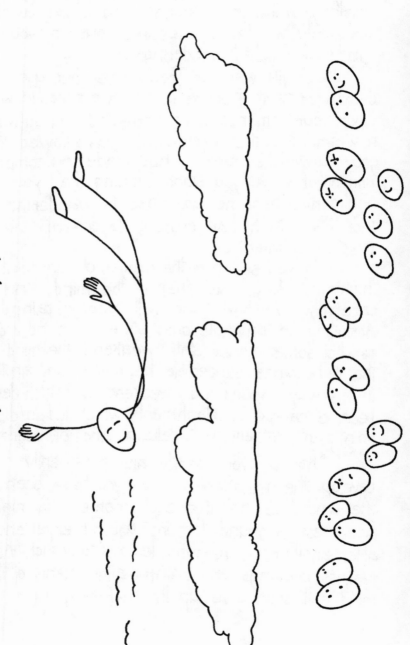

To be free we
must be comfortable
in being someone, anyone
or no one at any time
in any place

please remember...
everything which
has a beginning
has an ending

if we do not approach the matter of diet intelligently we will only constipate our minds. isn't freedom achieved when we can appreciatively accept any type of food that is offered?

attachment to any diet is spiritually poisonous. food in itself is not a means of transcendence. it only sustains the body while the mind works for its enlightenment.

we must sleep away one third of our
lives because
we wear ourselves out
liking and disliking
all day long

wise people are neither optimists
                              nor pessimists

they see things as they are...

each morning if we
commit ourselves to finding
the truth of every
situation
then miracles
come to us
all day long

when you find out who
you really are
it's beautiful
beyond your

dreams

is there
anything better
to be than
free?

when you're
flying
you can talk or not talk,
sing or not sing,
dance or not dance,
laugh or not laugh,
eat or not eat,
play or not play,
be serious or not be serious,
draw a picture or not
draw a picture
touch someone or not
touch someone
go or stay   live or die
and it all
tastes the same
joyful   joyful   joyful

karma means
intention

then action

everytime

you do a good karma
it comes back to you

prosperity

is

the result of kind living

money is always

helpful

it is not right to not want to be successful

get your but

out of the way

unbalanced reflections on the
negative things in life will depress you

at the end of the day
make a list of the good things
which happened to you

positive   negative

the buddhist does not :
     hurt things
     kill things
     harm things

the buddhist does :
     bless things with his love
     bring prosperity to all
     live happily and let live

     he is loved
     and cherished by his friends

buddhist precepts

no killing

no stealing

no lying

no intoxicants

no wrong sexual relations

some use alcohol, cigarettes or drugs

as a medicine for their mind

but as any medicine

too much is no good

neurotics depend on
holidays, weekends
and days-off

those who cultivate
their appreciation
celebrate
daily

control your mind
don't be under the control
of your mind ...

a human being
who controls his mind
is a saint

your closets

are

the mirror

of

your mind

relaxation

is

the only cure for

tension

say to yourself

I can learn to relax

irritation

is

natural

warts are

natural

too

express your love to your children

tell them everyday
how much you love them

express your love to everybody

anytime

express what you think

what you feel

always

with love

our relationships
are unfree to the
extent that we
demand things of
other people

love is not possessive

impeccable means:

making conscious choice
of what we eat, where we live,
our friends, our clothes,

our everything

the buddha was the most

compassionate

virtuous

loving

intelligent

informed

wellspoken

energetic

respecting

untense

prosperous

learned

refined

courageous

handsome

generosity is the number one prerequisite for progress on the spiritual path. without joyful and natural giving, there can be no recieving. the reason for this simple generosity is the direct expression, in action, of non-attachment. and non-attachment is the key to freedom from suffering.

like all virtues, generosity needs constant attention to flower and mature by regularly tithing a percentage of all your income to your point of inspiration, you can practice this in the most basic level - the material. the results of this will be immediately apparent in increased prosperity on all levels - (finances, meditation, relationships, emotions). and soon the act of giving itself becomes an experience of prosperity.

you can tithe from personal income. it will totally change the way you view your world. it will open you to living more fluidly and dynamically.

while we should give generously to those that need help, it is important that our first tithe regularly goes to our place of spiritual inspiration.

we must feed the fountain which nourishes our awakening wisdom.

where our tithe goes is a personal experience, something everyone must decide for himself.

tithing is putting your money where
your mouth is, about generosity

visākhā was a very generous lady, daughter of a millionaire, and the chief benefactress of the buddha. she regularly gave alms and tended to the monks living in the monastery.

one day she went to visit the buddha covered in her most valuable jewels and ornaments. on the way, she decided her dress was inappropriate and gave all her adornments to her servant for safe-keeping during the trip.

after hearing the buddha's discourse, visākhā returned home accompanied by the servant, who had forgotten the jewels and had left them at the gathering place in the monastery. ananda, the buddha's disciple and attendant, found the package and put it in a safe place for return to the lady.

when visākhā heard what had happened, she decided to use the opportunity to give a grand gift to the order. she thought first to give the jewels, then decided to sell them and use the money for things more suited to the use of monks. she then found that no one could afford such precious jewelry, so she decided to buy it herself, and use the money for the monks.

the buddha, pleased with her generosity, suggested she build a monastery, which she did. the buddha stayed there with his disciples for six rainy seasons.

rather than chastising her servant, visākhā was appreciative for the occasion to perform this meritorious deed.

the buddha's greatest supporter was anāthapindika, a wealthy businessman from sāvatthi. when anātha- pindika first heard of the buddha, a fully enligh- tened teacher in the world, his desire to meet him was very strong. rather than wait until the next day to visit, he traveled that night through the jungle, alone in total darkness to the place where the buddha was staying, and met him just before dawn.

upon receiving instruction from the buddha, his inspiration was so great that he invited the buddha to stay with him for the rains, along with the entire community of monks.

the buddha accepted, and anāthapindika set about finding a suitable place to build a monastery. he finally came upon the pleasure park of jeta, the prince of savatthi. now this park was a wonder- ful place, serene and peaceful and fulfilling all the requirements. a place such as this prince jeta was reluctant to lose, so he told anāthapindika the price would be determined by covering the entire grounds with gold coins, thinking this would deter him.

when anāthapindika started hauling in the gold in carts, jeta realized this was no ordinary purchase, and when the gold left a small spot uncovered, he gave that as his gift to the order of monks.

the monastery was constructed, and here the buddha spent the greater part of his life giving many discourses.

not only god loves

a cheerful giver

the gift of truth excels all gifts

there have been many
would be saviours
in the world

no one
has succeeded
in saving the world

save yourself

rather than trying to convince anybody
that meditation is the right path,
we can show by our attitude
(wisdom, mindfulness, happiness)
the benefits of meditation

believe nothing
merely because you have been
told it, or because it is
traditional, or because you
yourself have imagined it. do
not believe what your teacher
tells you, merely out of respect
for the teacher.

but whatever way by
thorough examination you find
to be one leading to good and
happiness for all creatures,

that path follow, like the
moon in the path
of stars

an american who began his search for understanding at an early age, sujata traveled half-way around the world where he found some very rare people who, unlike all others he had met, were not plagued by the universal human enslavements of hatred, attachment and selfishness.

using the tools of insight meditation which he practiced as a buddhist monk, sujata teaches meditators to watch carefully the ways of the mind. as resident teacher of stillpoint institute, he guides others along the buddha's path, through the difficult process of laying down the burden of self.

to those who want to study with
sujata please send your address,
phone number, and a donation to cover
a 20 min. call from san francisco to:

stillpoint institute
2740 greenwich # 416
san francisco, ca 94123

please make checks payable to
stillpoint institute   .
all contributions are tax- deductible

additional copies of beginning to see can
be ordered from Network
p.o. box 2246
berkeley, ca 94702
(415) 849-2665

enclose payment with order ($ 6.95 each book).
add $2.00 for postage and handling. california
residents must also include 6 % sales tax.

[OO] and [VISA] accepted. provide full information